THE INTERPRETER'S HOUSE

*The Chancellor's Installation Address
delivered before the University of
Edinburgh, July 20th 1938*

BY

THE RIGHT HONOURABLE

LORD TWEEDSMUIR
P.C., G.C.M.G., C.H., D.C.L., LL.D., D.LITT.

Governor-General of Canada

Copyright © 2013 Read Books Ltd.
This book is copyright and may not be
reproduced or copied in any way without
the express permission of the publisher in writing

British Library Cataloguing-in-Publication Data
A catalogue record for this book is available from the
British Library

John Buchan

John Buchan, first Baron Tweedsmuir of Elsfield, was born in Perth, Scotland in 1875. In his youth, his father immersed him in the history, legends and myths of Scotland, and he was an avid reader, stating some years later that John Bunyan's *The Pilgrim's Progress* was a "constant companion" to him. Buchan's education was uneven, but at the age of seventeen he obtained a scholarship to study classics at Glasgow University, where he began to write poetry. His first work, *The Essays and Apothegms of Francis Lord Bacon*, was published in 1894, and a year later he enrolled at Oxford University to study law.

In 1900, Buchan moved to London, and two years later accepted a civil service post in South Africa. In the years leading up to World War I, he worked at a publishers, and also wrote *Prester John* (1910) – which later became a school reader, translated into many languages – as well as a number of biographies. In 1915, Buchan became a war correspondent for *The Times*, and published his most well-known book, the thriller *The Thirty-Nine Steps*. After the war he became a director of the news agency Reuters.

Over the course of his life, Buchan would eventually publish some one hundred books, forty or so of which were novels, mostly wartime thrillers. In the latter part of his life he worked in politics, serving as Conservative MP for the Scottish universities and Lord High Commissioner of the Church of Scotland (1933-34). In 1935, Buchan moved to Canada, where he became the thirty-fifth Governor General of Canada. He died in 1940, aged 64.

THE INTERPRETER'S HOUSE

You have conferred upon me a great honour, and my first word to you must be an expression of deep gratitude. "To be the Chancellor of a University," Macaulay has written in his *History of England*, "was a distinction eagerly sought by the magnates of the realm. To represent a University in Parliament was a favourite object of the ambition of statesmen. Nobles and even princes were proud to receive from a University the privilege of wearing the doctoral scarlet." I am not a magnate and I have no claim to be called a statesman, but all three of the honours mentioned I have received at your hands. You have elected to your highest office one who is not a member of this famous seat of learning, one who, though in his day a student of a Scottish University, omitted—I blush to confess it—to proceed to a degree. But you are the centre of light and learning in a great city, that city is the metropolis of Scotland, and I think I can claim that I am idiomatically Scottish in descent and spirit. It is our business as we go through life to discover new loyalties. I am proud to think that to-day I have acquired a cause to which I can give whole-hearted devotion and service.

I am going to offer you this morning a few reflections on the meaning of a university. More years ago than he cares to count, he who now addresses you had his first sight of a university when he went to Glasgow for the Bursary examination. It was one of those flaming sunsets which in autumn sometimes illumine Gilmorehill, and its towers and pinnacles silhouetted against the western sky seemed to me like the battlements of a celestial city. There was a castellated gateway, I remember, and I felt as I entered it like Christian in *The Pilgrim's Progress*, with, on my back, a heavy load of imperfections. Well, unlike Bunyan's Pilgrim, I did not lose that burden. I soon ceased to regard Glasgow or any university as a goal, an end in itself, and the culmination of a pilgrimage. I thought of it rather as the Wicket Gate where the journey began. But I have come to think that an inept comparison. A university is not a mere wicket gate which, once passed, is no more thought of; it is something which should influence every stage of our life. So, adopting Bunyan's language, I think of it as the Interpreter's House where we receive our viaticum for the road.

I

A university has two plain duties. It has to transmit knowledge, and it has to advance knowledge. It has to transmit knowledge; that is to say it has to train the student's mind, and also to provide him with the special equipment which will enable him to earn a living; it has to give him as a basis a liberal education, and to add to that a professional technique. Both purposes require equal emphasis. A modicum of general culture will be of little value to a young man if he is going to starve. On the other hand, if we have only what has been called the "service-station" conception of a university we may have men entering a profession without having been taught to think, without possessing anything worth the name of mind. Our purpose is to combine humanism with technique.

By humanism I mean the study of man in all his relations, as thinker, as artist, as social and moral being; and by technique I mean the study of what might be called brute fact. Humanism is primarily a question of values. The object of humane studies is the understanding of human nature, the broadening of human interests and the better appreciation of the purpose of human life. Technique raises none of these questions. It is the mastery of brute fact for a definitely utilitarian end. Its concern is with material things and not with those of the spirit.

Now I believe that all true education requires a humane foundation. By humane learning I mean simply the disinterested pursuit of truth for its own sake, apart from any incidental advantages. The humanities should be broadly defined. They are not only art, literature, history, philosophy and religion; they are each and every science provided it is pursued in a certain way. There is a famous Cambridge toast that I have always liked: "God bless the higher mathematics and may they never be of the slightest use to anybody." It is not the subject matter which makes the distinction, for you can give humane value to any subject if you have the right attitude of mind.

The instruction of a university must be in the general principles, the fundamental propositions, the theory, of any discipline. It cannot profess to teach the practice of a profession, for it cannot keep step with its rapid changes. Therefore even on the side of technique the element of humanism should enter. If a technical training is regarded not merely as the acquisition of a certain number of rules of thumb but as a piece of serious mental discipline, then you are introducing the spirit of the humanities into the vocational side. You are producing not only technicians but men and women with minds. That is a point, you will remember, on which the Greek philosophers always insisted. One is inclined to think that the views of Aristotle and Plato on education were highly unpractical—the sort of thing which would be well enough in a small leisured city, but which is meaningless in the crowded world of to-day. You remember that they were always condemning the occupations which they called mechanical, and which we honour to-day under the names of commercial and technical. Yes; but there is a passage in Aristotle's *Politics* in which he seems to me to talk excellent good sense. It is the object, he says, which a man sets before him in his study which makes the difference. If he does or learns anything for its own sake, or with a view to the development of his mind and character, then that pursuit, whatever its subject, will be a liberal education.

I have given you a rough definition of the educational purpose of a university. But there is the other not less vital aspect of its work, the protection and the advancement of knowledge. We must regard it not only as a seminary for the training of youth, but as a museum for record, a laboratory for discovery, a power-house for inspiration. The two duties are closely united, for unless they have a centre of creative thought behind them the various professions for which we train our youth will become stagnant and blind.

So one should regard, I think, as a primary function of a university the trusteeship of humane learning, the guardianship of the central culture of mankind. Its task is to pursue truth by research, by experiment and by speculation, and in so doing to inspire its members, young and old, with the love of truth, which includes the love of beauty, and with that spirit of disinterested enquiry which means intellectual freedom. In this work it will do far more than instruct in the narrow sense, for it will enable youth to instruct itself—in the words of a famous Cambridge scholar, "to seek out themselves, and to seek with an exacting conscience." Without this high and serious purpose a university is only sounding brass and a tinkling cymbal. This was the task of the academies of Greece amid the dynastic wars of the ancient world. It was the task of the universities of Europe in the Dark Ages when learning was a series of pin-pricks of light, zealously tended in the gloom and confusion. It has been the task of modern universities to keep the flame pure when an era of progress has kindled so many murky fires. It is our task especially to-day, when obscurity threatens many of the lights we cherish. To change the metaphor, a university is like one of our Border castles that stood on the highway from England. The duty of such a castle was not only to safeguard its adjacent territory but to hold the pass against invasion and from its battlements to flash a warning far afield.

II

You will, I hope, forgive these platitudes. They are a necessary prologue to my argument, but they are only a formal statement of a university's purpose. For behind them lies the intimate and most human duty of starting youth on its career. We are not dealing with inanimate counters, but with living, breathing human beings on whom the future of the nation depends. We must give them the elements of a liberal education, we must give them the rudiments of a professional technique, we must enlist their services in the pursuit of truth and the safeguarding of knowledge. We must adapt them and adapt ourselves to the circumstances of a most difficult world, a world where, as it seems to many, the foundations are

THE INTERPRETER'S HOUSE

crumbling. What have we to say to the youth of to-day?

Let me first of all suggest to you what I think we cannot say. We cannot ask them to retrace their steps. There is a movement in America at present which I have been watching with deep interest, a movement not without parallels in the Old World. It is partly due to what I think is the acknowledged failure of the practice of giving students too wide a choice in the contents of a curriculum. Under that practice a young man was permitted to make his own selection from a huge variety of subjects; the result was that his training tended to be in snippets, which collectively did not represent a true intellectual discipline. The intention was honest, for it was designed to bring a flavour of the practical into all his studies, but this slender utilitarian interest did not dignify topics which had intrinsically small educational worth. The movement is also partly due to the recent revival of interest in the philosophy of St. Thomas Aquinas, a revival for which I have only praise, and in which I am glad to think that Canada is taking a leading part.

What is the gospel of these modern Thomists? The present system, they say, is chaos, and we must bring out of it a cosmos. The first business of education is to build up a mind, and that can only be done by a rigorous and systematic training. Therefore we must go back to the custom of our forefathers, who based all learning on the study of philosophy. In the University of Salerno, the chief medical school in the Europe of the Middle Ages, before beginning his medical course a student had to spend three years in the study of logic and metaphysics. We must return to the teaching of philosophy as our basis, and whatever system of philosophy we choose it must be a complete system, an absolute system, a system of first principles.

Now I confess that, while I have every sympathy with the purpose of these reformers, I am very doubtful about their method. Beyond doubt a strict education in a closed system of thought—for example, the scholastic logic which used to be part of our Scottish curriculum—is a far better training for the mind than to permit it to wander among snippets of knowledge. But is it the best? Is it indeed a possible one to-day? One difficulty is as to which of the older philosophical systems should be chosen. A greater difficulty is how you would link it up with the multitudinous intellectual activities of the modern world, the study of the physical universe and of the infinite ramifications of human society. Would it not tend to become a mere riveted chain of dogmas, barren, in Bacon's famous words, like a virgin consecrated to God? It was very well in earlier days to make a theology or a metaphysic the foundation of all study, but that was possible because these were universally accepted creeds already interwoven with men's thoughts and dreams, and not adopted coldly as an educational method. To return to them would be to treat an intermediate stage in human thought as the final stage. It would give us order, no doubt, but would it not be a dead and empty order? I remember a pregnant saying of Professor Whitehead's: "A self-satisfied rationalism is in effect a form of anti-rationalism. It means an arbitrary halt at a particular set of abstractions."

I have said that I sympathise with the purpose of these modern Thomists, and I think I understand their motive. They hunger, as we all hunger, for a greater security. They envy the Middle Ages their well-defined forms of thought and their well-rounded cosmogony. It is a desire which must always come upon a people in a time of violent change. It came upon the Greeks when their confidence was shaken. . . . But it is apt to have calamitous consequences. In Athens it led to the death of Socrates. . . . To select arbitrarily a set of first principles, and to make all our studies subordinate to them, is in effect to establish an intellectual dictatorship and to kill the freedom of the mind. It is true that it would give us orderliness, but it would be the orderliness of death.

To-day, when there is so much anarchy abroad, the spirit of man, which detests anarchy, is willing to pay a high price for the return of law. We have seen great nations for this reason surrender their ancient liberties to a man or a machine. But too high a price can be paid for order. If we have in our intellectual world to-day much confusion, we have also a rich promise. "Where no oxen are the crib is clean, but much increase is by the strength of the ox." I would suggest what seems to me to be a wiser attitude. It is not a chain of dogmas to which we should return, but an insistence upon the liberty and sacrosanctity of the mind. We are plagued to-day by an epidemic of anti-rationalism. The human reason is not a perfect thing, but it is the best we have, and it is our duty to reverence it and give it free play. It is anti-rationalism to find a mystical virtue in half-baked "ideologies"—if I may use a new piece of jargon; it is anti-rationalism—"escapism," to employ the same jargon—to fly for shelter to an old building of our forefathers which is remote from the true arena of conflict. Two things we must zealously defend, the freedom and the integrity of our thought, boldly facing new conditions, ready to meet any problem, shirking no difficulty, but rigid in our fidelity to the laws which govern our intellectual being. Only thus shall we find confusion give place to order, and it will be the order of a harvest-field and not of a graveyard.

III

I come back to what must dominate all our purposes—our human material, our youth. If we can give them minds accustomed to think and inspired with a reverence for thought, and at the same time give them the perspective created by some understanding of our long human story, then we have endowed them with what is most needed—confidence and hope. I hear to-day from many quarters foolish jeremiads about the younger generation; jeremiads which are not deep calling to deep, but shallow moaning to shallow. We are told that they lack the enterprise, the stamina and the fortitude of their fathers. That I believe to be wholly untrue. I have always regarded my own undergraduate generation as vigorous and enterprising, but it seems to me that the present generation has a physical audacity which would have left us gasping. A few years ago I made a note of how some of my son's contemporaries were spending their Oxford long vacation, and I found the following:— deck-hand in a Hull trawler in the White Sea; working at the Canadian harvest; purser in a South American liner; helping Welsh miners to cultivate the land; trading old rifles in the Arctic for walrus ivory. It is as though they felt that they were living in a hard and dangerous world, and were resolved that there should be no experience which they could not face.

And I think that they have a like intellectual boldness. They seem to me to feel their responsibility to the State more keenly than my own contemporaries, and they look on politics as a serious personal duty. Youth is prone to extremes, and it is small wonder that the causes which appeal to many are the new grandiose world-reconstructions. If youth were not interested in such creeds then it would no longer be young. Its inclination towards extremes is due, I think, not only to the rhetorical turn of youth, but to the fact that such causes demand sacrifices and an austere discipline. Moreover, they are clean-cut and confident, and, in the prevailing confusion, youth demands something firm on which it can lay hold. If the universities are to fulfil their duty and marry the forward-looking spirit to the wisdom of the past, they must be not less bold and positive and confident. Like the Scriptural householder, they must bring from their stores things new as well as things old.

But if the spirit of adventure is as alive to-day as ever, has it the same food to feed on? Since I was an undergraduate the globe is sadly shrunken. Forty years ago there was a big back-world of mystery waiting for the discoverer. The west of the North American continent was still largely unsettled. The maps of Central Asia and Central Africa were full of blank spaces. Lhasa was unvisited. The holy cities of Islam were forbidden places. Only the fringe of the Polar regions had been travelled in. . . . To-day we know all about Lhasa and Mecca and Medina. We have visited the North and the South Poles. The mystery mountain ranges have been explored, the Arctic giants of Alaska have been climbed, and the equatorial snows of the Mountains of the Moon. If we have not yet conquered Everest we have prospected all of it. The desert of Southern Arabia has been crossed, and the gorges of the Bramaputra have been traversed. There are no major geographical riddles left, and most of the unknown patches on the map are now well within the orbit of human knowledge and human enterprise.

That is true, but it is not the whole truth. If the great riddles have been solved there remains an infinity of lesser puzzles. Our business now is less discovery than development. Take the Canadian North. It is nearly a century and a half since Alexander Mackenzie reached the Arctic; it is nearly a century since the first surveys were made on the shores of the Polar Sea. To-day the work is still going on, it is still pioneering, but it is intensive and detailed. We are founding settlements and winning natural wealth inside the Arctic Circle, and giving to what was a mere geographical expression the apparatus of civilised life. There are still many physical frontiers in the world, border-lines beyond which lies the little known.

But, more important, there are the

spiritual frontiers, the horizons of the mind. We are still frontiersmen in a true sense, for we are domiciled on the edge of mystery, and have to face novelties more startling than any which confronted the old pioneers. Our youth, living on a spiritual frontier, still needs all the audacity and fortitude of the pioneer. As I see it, there is ample room for the spirit of adventure and for the discipline behind it which makes adventure fruitful.

IV

My word to-day is therefore less to the wise men who are responsible for the administration of this University—they know their business and their duties far better than I do—than to the young men who come to this Interpreter's House to be equipped for the journey. I can put it in one sentence. They have a more difficult task than their fathers, they are called to a severer test, a more momentous duty, but they have a greater opportunity to prove the virtue that is in them.

First for those who after their university course will enter one of the normal vocations—the Church, medicine, the law, industry or commerce. They will find the technique of their profession more elaborate than in their fathers' day; the Church has to confront a more critical world, medicine has a more intricate subject matter, the lawyer has to face a multitude of novel problems, the business man has to operate a more complex machine. But I am concerned less with their professional difficulties than with the problems which, as educated and civilised men, they will have to face—the new duties of citizenship. The citizen of a nation like ours has to-day a peculiar responsibility. If he is true to the spirit of his university he has to help to maintain that delicate structure which we call civilisation, in the face of a world which is full of destructive forces. In the last two centuries mankind has advanced far on the road to toleration, one of the first of the civic virtues; but now an intolerant spirit is abroad which claims for this or that dogma the status of final truth, and would compel its acceptance by fire and sword. We are in danger of a return of the old wars of religion. Aristotle called man a "political animal"; there are too many to-day who would put the emphasis on the word "animal."

Again, the mechanism of the State has become most intricate, and at the same time it bulks far more largely in the life of the ordinary man. Therefore if a free polity is to succeed it must be as efficient as any authoritarian regime, and that means for all of us a greater measure of public spirit, a greater effort to subordinate private to public good, a quickened interest and a stronger intelligence in public affairs. It is easy to devise an authoritarian machine which will appear to be more effective than the patient methods of democracy. We have the task of proving that those short cuts are illusory and that freedom does not mean ineptitude. We have to purge the defects and confirm the virtues of our democracy; we have to show that human nature is worthy of freedom. Such a task makes high demands upon patience and wisdom and good temper; it needs the best kind of courage, not the bravado of the swashbuckler, but the fortitude of the citizen. Our liberties, which we took for granted, have now become a cause to fight for; the truths, which once seemed platitudes, are now the oriflamme of a crusade. Could there be a nobler challenge to youth? My old friend F. S. Oliver, an alumnus of Edinburgh, has described the work of the statesman as an "endless adventure." The task to-day of every educated man may be called an endless adventure.

In the second place, there are students who will give their lives not to a profession, but to the university's prime duty, the advancement of knowledge by some form of research. Scientific research to-day has reached a height undreamed of before, and has become not a hobby, or a luxury, but an imperious necessity. We are the slaves of our own successes. A congested population in certain areas which has to be fed from overseas; a higher standard of living; industries depending upon foreign supplies of raw material—these and a hundred other factors compel us to keep the scientific apparatus we have devised at the highest pitch of efficiency, and to be always extending and improving it. Again, our life has become elaborately specialised. A man is no longer master of several crafts, but of one only, and that involves an intricate system of co-operation, which must be invulnerable or the result is chaos.

What does this mean? That, just because our mechanism is so intricate, it is far more exposed to disaster than the simpler mechanism of earlier days. We can only preserve the standard which we have set ourselves by the constant exertion of intelligence. It means that scientists must be always on the watch to discover newer and better processes of production and distribution. It means that industry must be quick to make use of the results of such research and to adopt new methods.

To-day the work is widely ramified. It is undertaken by the intelligence departments of certain great industries. It is undertaken by the State, either directly or by grants of public money. I would instance in Britain the National Physical Laboratory, the Biological Survey, the Medical Research Council, and the Agricultural Research Council, and in Canada the National Council of Scientific Research. These organisations are doing brilliant work. For example, there was a certain piece of electrical research recently completed in Britain at a cost of some eighty thousand pounds, the result of which has been the saving to the electrical industry of a million pounds per annum; and I could parallel this from Canadian experience. I believe that if a profit-and-loss account of these activities were made up on true lines it would be found that they were making many hundreds per cent. for the nation on their capital outlay. I want to see the State extend its interests in this direction, for there is no more fruitful public service. But the task cannot be confined to the State and to private enterprise; it must be in a very special degree the work of the universities. It is a fulfilment of one of their principal duties, the advancement of knowledge.

Young men, I hope, will make this their life-work in increasing numbers, whether in the service of the universities, of industry, or of the State. I cannot imagine a more engrossing profession. In the first place, it has the highest purpose, the pursuit of truth, the unfettered exercise of the human reason. In the second place, it is a work of profound public importance, and the men and women who undertake it are in the fullest sense servants of the State. In the third place, it offers a life which can never be dull, for it is a life of perpetual adventure. You can never tell what small by-product of your enquiries may not turn out to be an epoch-making discovery. " The more thou searchest," to quote the inscription on the headquarters of the Research Council in Ottawa, " the more thou shalt marvel." There can be nothing narrow and stereotyped about a task which is a continuous fruitful groping into the unknown. A traveller often goes furthest when he is least certain of his goal. I remember a saying of Emeritus President Lowell of Harvard: "Columbus," he said, "when he set out did not know where he was going. When he arrived he did not know where he was. When he returned he did not know where he had been. But all the same he discovered America."

There is one branch of research which I should like to commend to your attention, research in that group of subjects which deal with social relations, and which, in a not very happy translation of the German *Sozialwissenschaft*, we call the "social sciences." Obviously research in these is very different from research in the physical world. The data are more confused, the chances of laboratory work are rarer. We have not the same power of making experiments and reaching the truth by trial and error. But, difficult as it is, research is possible on the same principles as in physical science, and I want to see more of it. At present we are inclined to attach high importance to these social studies, but we have not gone far in the development of a method. We laboriously and rather indiscriminately accumulate data on every kind of topic—population, crime, poverty, unemployment, the incidence of taxation, migration—there is no end to the list. But the data are apt to remain undigested, unrelated, and therefore meaningless. Shelley's words in his *Defence of Poetry* are only too true. "We have more moral, political and historical wisdom," he says, "than we know how to reduce into practice.... Our calculations have outrun our conception; we have eaten more than we can digest." We have piled up the ore but we have still to smelt it. We need fewer collectors and more interpreters—men and women who will use their trained intelligence as well as their industry. I hope for good results from the new Nuffield College at Oxford, and from the body of workers which Lord Stamp has got together to be a kind of general staff for social studies. It is a field in which every university can do fruitful work.

V

To produce minds, which are not ammunition dumps but guns to fire off ammunition; to give these minds a practical training for whatever vocation they choose, and a liberal background which will enable them to use the bequest of the past; to inspire our youth so that they may hail with enthusiasm the duties and the opportunities which await them—could a loftier task be entrusted to any human fraternity? Let me conclude these random observations in the fashion of our Scottish ancestors, with two appropriate prayers, for in these difficult days our reflections must usually end in prayer. The first is from Plato. There is a beautiful passage at the close of the *Phaedrus* when Socrates and Phaedrus, after discussing many things, turn homeward in the afternoon. But before they leave the grove by the Ilissus, Socrates observes that one should not leave the haunt of Pan without a prayer. And this is his prayer. "Oh, auspicious Pan, and ye other deities of this place, grant to me to become beautiful inwardly, and that all my outward goods may prosper my inner soul." The second is the words of Queen Elizabeth when, on her last visit, she looked back at Oxford from Shotover hill. "Farewell, farewell, dear Oxford! God bless thee and increase thy sons in number, in holiness, and in virtue."

With these kindred prayers, your Chancellor for the present takes his leave of this University.

www.ingramcontent.com/pod-product-compliance
Lightning Source LLC
Chambersburg PA
CBHW022127090426
42743CB00008B/1044